Choosing the Right Business for Financial Freedom

C. P. Kumar
Reiki Healer & Author
Roorkee - 247667, India

Disclaimer

While every effort has been made to ensure the accuracy and completeness of the content in this book, the author cannot guarantee that the information contained herein is error-free, up-to-date, or suitable for every individual circumstance.

The author shall not be held liable or responsible for any errors or omissions in the content of the book, nor for any damages, or losses that may arise from any actions taken based upon the suggestions or contents presented in the book.

Readers are advised to use their own judgment and discretion in applying the information provided in this book, and to consult with qualified professionals before taking any action based on the contents of this book. The author disclaims any and all liability or responsibility for any actions taken or not taken based on the information contained in this book.

DEDICATION

To all aspiring entrepreneurs who dare to dream, and to those who tirelessly pursue financial freedom, this book is dedicated to you.

May the chapters within these pages be your guiding light as you embark on the journey of choosing the right business for your prosperity and fulfillment. In every chapter lies wisdom and insight, crafted to empower your decisions and nurture your entrepreneurial spirit.

May you find inspiration in the challenges you face and courage in the risks you take, for greatness lies within your reach. With gratitude to those who have walked this path before and with anticipation for those who will follow, this dedication is but a token of our shared journey.

Here's to the dreamers, the doers, and the visionaries. May your endeavors bring you not only wealth but also purpose, joy, and lasting impact.

C. P. Kumar

CONTENTS

PREFACE

In today's dynamic and ever-evolving economic landscape, the pursuit of financial freedom through entrepreneurship has become both an enticing opportunity and a daunting challenge. As individuals, we aspire to carve our paths, build legacies, and secure our financial futures. Yet, amidst the myriad of options and possibilities, choosing the right business venture can seem like navigating a labyrinth without a map.

This book, "Choosing the Right Business for Financial Freedom", emerges as a beacon amidst this complexity, offering guidance, insight, and practical wisdom to those embarking on the exhilarating journey of entrepreneurship. Within these pages, we delve deep into the intricacies of selecting the business venture that aligns with your passions, skills, and aspirations.

We explore fundamental aspects of self-awareness and mindset, helping you assess your readiness for the entrepreneurial voyage. From there, we embark on a journey of self-discovery, exploring how to identify your passion, leverage your skills, and find the perfect fit for your entrepreneurial endeavor.

As we traverse through the landscape of business opportunities, we delve into the importance of market research, risk assessment, and reward evaluation. We explore the diverse array of business models, from service-based enterprises to product-driven ventures, empowering you to choose the structure that resonates with your vision and values.

In the digital age, we recognize the paramount significance of technology, innovation, and digital presence. Yet, amidst the allure of innovation, we anchor ourselves in the practicalities of financing, legal compliance, and team building.

With a steadfast focus on sustainability, integrity, and growth, we navigate through the realms of branding, marketing, customer relationship management, and financial stewardship. Along the way, we embrace the inevitability of setbacks and failures, recognizing them as catalysts for growth and resilience.

As stewards of the future, we espouse the ethos of sustainability and social responsibility, exploring the delicate balance between profit and purpose. And as we chart our course towards the horizon, we confront the prospect of exits and legacies, planning for the future with foresight and intentionality.

Through a synthesis of practical insights, real-world examples, and actionable strategies, this book endeavors to equip you with the knowledge, tools, and confidence to embark on your entrepreneurial odyssey. Whether you are a seasoned entrepreneur seeking new horizons or an aspiring visionary ready to take the plunge, "Choosing the Right Business for Financial Freedom" serves as your trusted companion, illuminating the path towards prosperity, fulfillment, and enduring success.

May this book inspire, empower, and guide you as you embark on the transformative journey of entrepreneurship, forging a future defined by purpose, passion, and prosperity.

C. P. Kumar
Reiki Healer & Author
Former Scientist 'G', National Institute of Hydrology
Roorkee - 247667, India
Web: https://www.angelfire.com/nh/cpkumar/virgo.html

Introduction

In the pursuit of financial freedom through entrepreneurship, one of the most crucial elements to consider is your mindset. The entrepreneurial journey is rife with challenges, uncertainties, and opportunities, and your readiness to navigate these waters can significantly impact your chances of success. Before diving headfirst into any business venture, it's essential to assess your entrepreneurial mindset and determine if you're adequately prepared for the road ahead.

Defining the Entrepreneurial Mindset

At its core, the entrepreneurial mindset encompasses a unique set of attitudes, beliefs, and behaviors that drive individuals to identify opportunities, take calculated risks, and persist in the face of adversity. Unlike traditional employees, entrepreneurs often thrive in environments where uncertainty and ambiguity reign supreme. They possess a relentless drive to innovate, problem-solve, and create value in the marketplace.

Traits of Successful Entrepreneurs

Successful entrepreneurs exhibit a myriad of traits that set them apart from the average individual. These traits include:

1. Resilience

Entrepreneurship is fraught with setbacks, failures, and unforeseen challenges. Resilient entrepreneurs possess the ability to bounce back from adversity, learn from their mistakes, and adapt their strategies accordingly. They view failures not as roadblocks but as valuable learning experiences on the path to success.

2. Vision

Visionary entrepreneurs possess a clear sense of purpose and direction for their ventures. They can envision the future they want to create and formulate strategic plans to turn their vision into reality. A compelling vision serves as a guiding light, motivating entrepreneurs to stay focused and committed to their goals, even when the going gets tough.

3. Creativity

Creativity lies at the heart of entrepreneurship. Successful entrepreneurs possess the ability to think outside the box, challenge the status quo, and generate innovative solutions to complex problems. They embrace experimentation and are not afraid to explore unconventional ideas in pursuit of differentiation and competitive advantage.

4. Adaptability

In today's fast-paced business landscape, adaptability is key to survival. Successful entrepreneurs possess the flexibility to pivot their strategies, adjust to changing market conditions, and capitalize on emerging trends. They are quick to recognize shifts in consumer preferences and industry dynamics, allowing them to stay ahead of the curve and maintain relevance in the marketplace.

5. Passion

Passion fuels the entrepreneurial spirit. Successful entrepreneurs are deeply passionate about their ventures, products, or services. They believe wholeheartedly in what they're doing and are willing to invest the time, energy, and resources necessary to bring their vision to fruition. Passion not only sustains entrepreneurs through the inevitable ups and downs but also inspires others to rally behind their cause.

Assessing Your Entrepreneurial Readiness

Before embarking on your entrepreneurial journey, it's essential to conduct a thorough self-assessment to gauge your readiness for the challenges that lie ahead. Consider the following factors:

1. Personal Motivation

Reflect on your reasons for wanting to become an entrepreneur. Are you driven by a genuine passion for your chosen industry or market? Do you possess a burning desire to solve a specific problem or meet an unmet need? Your personal motivation will serve as the foundation of your entrepreneurial journey and will sustain you through the inevitable obstacles you'll encounter along the way.

2. Risk Tolerance

Entrepreneurship inherently involves risk. Assess your tolerance for uncertainty and your willingness to take calculated risks in pursuit of your goals. Are you comfortable stepping outside your comfort zone and embracing the unknown? Successful entrepreneurs understand that risk is an inherent part of the game and are willing to accept the possibility of failure in exchange for the potential rewards that await them.

3. Financial Preparedness

Launching and growing a business requires a significant financial investment. Assess your current financial situation and determine if you have the resources necessary to fund your venture. Consider your savings, access to capital, and willingness to take on debt if needed. A solid financial foundation will provide you with the stability and flexibility to weather the inevitable financial challenges that accompany entrepreneurship.

4. Skills and Expertise

Evaluate your skills, knowledge, and expertise relevant to your chosen industry or market. Identify areas where you excel and areas where you may need to develop additional competencies. Surround yourself with mentors, advisors, and industry experts who can provide guidance and support as you navigate the complexities of entrepreneurship. Continuous learning and skill development are essential ingredients for long-term success in the business world.

5. Support Network

Entrepreneurship can be a lonely journey, but it doesn't have to be. Cultivate a strong support network of family, friends, mentors, and fellow entrepreneurs who can offer encouragement, advice, and perspective when you need it most. Surround yourself with positive influences who believe in your vision and are invested in your success.

Conclusion

Assessing your entrepreneurial mindset and readiness is a critical first step in the journey toward financial freedom through entrepreneurship. By understanding your strengths, weaknesses, motivations, and risk tolerance, you can better position yourself for success and mitigate the challenges that lie ahead. Remember, entrepreneurship is not for the faint of heart, but for those who possess the passion, resilience, and vision to turn their dreams into reality. As you embark on this exciting adventure, embrace the journey, celebrate the victories, and learn from the inevitable setbacks along the way. With the right mindset and readiness, the possibilities are endless.

This article lays the groundwork for aspiring entrepreneurs to understand the importance of assessing their mindset and readiness before diving into the world of business. It sets the stage for the subsequent chapters that will delve deeper into the process of choosing the right business for financial freedom.

Introduction

In the pursuit of financial freedom, choosing the right business is paramount. Yet, amidst the plethora of options, finding the perfect fit can be challenging. It requires a deep understanding of oneself, including passions, skills, and interests. This article delves into the process of identifying your passion and skills to find the ideal business opportunity that aligns with your strengths and aspirations.

Understanding Passion

Passion is the driving force that ignites our enthusiasm and fuels our commitment. It's what makes the difference between simply working and truly thriving in what we do. Identifying your passion involves introspection and exploration. Reflect on activities that bring you joy and fulfillment. What subjects or hobbies captivate your interest? What could you do for hours without feeling drained? Your passion often lies at the intersection of what you love and what you excel at.

Exploring Your Skills

Skills are the tools that enable us to turn our passion into tangible results. They encompass both innate talents and acquired knowledge. Take inventory of your skills by assessing your strengths, weaknesses, and areas of expertise. Consider your professional experience, education, and training. What tasks do you perform effortlessly? Where do others seek your advice or assistance? Recognizing your skills empowers you to leverage them effectively in your business endeavors.

Identifying Market Opportunities

Once you have a clear understanding of your passion and skills, explore potential market opportunities. Analyze industry trends, consumer demands, and emerging niches. Where does your passion intersect with market needs? Are there gaps or underserved segments that align with your expertise? Conduct thorough market research to identify viable business ideas that resonate with your interests and capabilities.

Assessing Viability and Sustainability

While passion and skills are essential, they must be complemented by a realistic assessment of business viability and sustainability. Evaluate the market dynamics, competitive landscape, and financial considerations. Is there sufficient demand for your product or service? What are the barriers to entry, and how will you differentiate yourself? Assess the long-term potential and scalability of your business concept to ensure its sustainability over time.

Seeking Alignment with Values and Goals

Beyond financial considerations, it's crucial to align your business venture with your values and long-term goals. Define what success means to you beyond monetary gains. How does your business contribute to your personal fulfillment and sense of purpose? Consider factors such as work-life balance, social impact, and environmental sustainability. Building a business that resonates with your values fosters greater satisfaction and fulfillment along the entrepreneurial journey.

Embracing Adaptability and Growth

In the dynamic landscape of entrepreneurship, adaptability and continuous learning are essential virtues. Remain open to feedback, challenges, and opportunities for growth. Embrace failure as a stepping stone to success and view setbacks as learning experiences. Cultivate a mindset of resilience and flexibility as you navigate the complexities of business ownership. Embrace innovation and stay attuned to evolving market trends to adapt your strategies accordingly.

Developing a Personalized Business Plan

Armed with insights into your passion, skills, and market opportunities, it's time to develop a personalized business plan. Define your mission, vision, and unique value proposition. Outline your target market, competitive analysis, and marketing strategies. Establish clear objectives, milestones, and key performance indicators to measure your progress. A well-crafted business plan serves as a roadmap for success and guides your decision-making process.

Fostering a Supportive Network

Entrepreneurship can be a solitary journey, but it doesn't have to be. Surround yourself with a supportive network of mentors, advisors, and fellow entrepreneurs. Seek guidance from industry experts and leverage their insights to navigate challenges and seize opportunities. Participate in networking events, workshops, and online communities to expand your connections and learn from others' experiences. Building a strong support system fosters collaboration, innovation, and personal growth.

Taking Action and Iterating

Ultimately, the path to finding the right business for financial freedom requires action and iteration. Take calculated risks and don't let fear of failure deter you from pursuing your dreams. Start small, test your ideas, and gather feedback from customers and stakeholders. Be prepared to iterate and refine your business model based on real-world insights and market feedback. Success rarely comes overnight, but with perseverance and determination, you can turn your passion and skills into a thriving enterprise.

Conclusion

Identifying the right business opportunity is a deeply personal and introspective journey. It requires a blend of self-awareness, market acumen, and strategic planning. By aligning your passion and skills with market opportunities, you can create a business that not only generates financial rewards but also brings fulfillment and purpose to your life. Stay true to your vision, embrace challenges as opportunities for growth, and never underestimate the transformative power of following your passion.

Chapter 3. Market Research Essentials
Analyzing Trends and Opportunities

Introduction

In the dynamic landscape of business, market research stands as a cornerstone for success. Understanding market trends and identifying opportunities are crucial steps in establishing a sustainable and profitable business. Whether you're a budding entrepreneur or a seasoned business owner, grasping the essentials of market research can pave the way for informed decision-making and long-term growth. In this article, we delve into the fundamental aspects of market research, focusing on analyzing trends and seizing opportunities to achieve financial freedom.

Understanding Market Trends

Market trends represent the prevailing direction or pattern of consumer behavior, industry developments, and economic factors that influence purchasing decisions. Analyzing market trends provides valuable insights into the demands, preferences, and shifts in consumer behavior within a particular industry or market segment. Here are key considerations for understanding market trends.

1. Consumer Behavior Analysis

Consumer behavior is the bedrock of market trends. By studying consumer preferences, purchasing patterns, and lifestyle choices, businesses can anticipate market shifts and tailor their offerings to meet evolving demands. Analyzing consumer behavior involves gathering data through surveys, focus groups, and social listening tools to decipher buying motives and preferences.

2. Industry Research

Industry research involves examining macroeconomic indicators, competitive landscapes, and regulatory factors impacting a specific sector. Businesses must stay abreast of industry developments, technological advancements, and emerging trends to adapt their strategies accordingly. Conducting SWOT (Strengths, Weaknesses, Opportunities, Threats) analyses can aid in identifying market gaps and competitive advantages.

3. Technological Innovations

The rapid pace of technological innovation shapes market dynamics and disrupts traditional business models. Keeping abreast of technological advancements enables businesses to leverage new tools, platforms, and digital channels to enhance customer experiences and streamline operations. Embracing innovation fosters agility and competitiveness in an increasingly digital marketplace.

Identifying Market Opportunities

Market opportunities arise from unmet needs, untapped segments, and emerging niches within the market ecosystem. Identifying and capitalizing on market opportunities require proactive research, strategic planning, and a keen understanding of consumer insights. Here are key strategies for identifying market opportunities.

1. Gap Analysis

Conducting gap analysis involves identifying discrepancies between consumer needs and existing products or services in the market. By pinpointing unmet needs or pain points, businesses can innovate and develop solutions that resonate with their target audience. *Pain points* refer to specific problems or challenges experienced by individuals or groups that cause discomfort, dissatisfaction, or inconvenience in a particular context or situation. Market gaps present fertile ground for entrepreneurial ventures and product differentiation strategies.

2. Competitive Analysis

Analyzing competitors' strengths, weaknesses, and market positioning provides valuable intelligence for identifying gaps and differentiation opportunities. *Differentiation opportunities* are distinct characteristics or strategies that enable a product, service, or brand to stand out and distinguish itself from competitors within a market or industry. By benchmarking against competitors and conducting comparative analyses, businesses can uncover underserved market segments or areas ripe for disruption. Understanding competitor strategies informs strategic decision-making and helps businesses carve out their unique value proposition.

3. Emerging Trends and Demographics

Anticipating future trends and demographic shifts enables businesses to align their offerings with evolving consumer preferences and lifestyle choices. Monitoring demographic trends, cultural shifts, and socio-economic factors empowers businesses to tailor their marketing messages and product offerings to resonate with diverse audience segments. Embracing diversity and inclusivity fosters brand loyalty and strengthens market positioning in an increasingly multicultural society.

Harnessing Data Analytics

Data analytics serves as a powerful tool for extracting actionable insights from vast datasets and informing strategic decision-making. Leveraging advanced analytics techniques such as predictive modeling, customer segmentation, and data visualization enables businesses to derive meaningful patterns and trends from disparate sources. Here's how data analytics can enhance market research efforts.

1. Predictive Modeling

Predictive modeling utilizes historical data and statistical algorithms to forecast future trends, customer behavior, and market dynamics. By analyzing past trends and identifying predictive variables, businesses can anticipate market shifts, mitigate risks, and capitalize on emerging opportunities. Predictive modeling empowers businesses to make data-driven decisions and optimize resource allocation for maximum impact.

2. Customer Segmentation

Customer segmentation involves categorizing customers based on shared characteristics, behaviors, and preferences. By segmenting customers into distinct groups, businesses can tailor their marketing strategies, product offerings, and pricing strategies to meet the unique needs of each segment. Customer segmentation enhances personalization, improves customer engagement, and drives conversion rates across diverse audience segments.

3. Data Visualization

Data visualization transforms complex datasets into intuitive charts, graphs, and dashboards that facilitate insights discovery and decision-making. Visualizing key metrics and trends enables stakeholders to identify patterns, outliers, and correlations within the data, leading to informed strategic initiatives and performance optimization. Data visualization tools such as Tableau, Power BI, and Google Data Studio empower businesses to communicate insights effectively and drive organizational alignment. They are used for transforming raw data into visually appealing and interactive dashboards and reports, each with its own unique features, strengths, and user interfaces catering to various data analysis needs and preferences.

Conclusion

Market research serves as a compass for navigating the ever-evolving landscape of business, guiding entrepreneurs and businesses towards profitable opportunities and sustainable growth. By understanding market trends, identifying opportunities, and harnessing the power of data analytics, businesses can gain a competitive edge, foster innovation, and achieve financial freedom. Embracing a proactive approach to market research enables businesses to anticipate market shifts, capitalize on emerging trends, and cultivate lasting relationships with customers in an increasingly dynamic marketplace. In the pursuit of financial freedom, market research stands as an indispensable ally, empowering businesses to chart a course towards success amidst uncertainty and change.

Introduction

In the realm of entrepreneurship and investment, risk and reward are two sides of the same coin. Every decision to start a business or invest capital involves a careful consideration of the potential risks and the expected rewards. Understanding your risk tolerance is crucial in making informed decisions that align with your financial goals and personal comfort level. In this article, we'll delve into the intricacies of assessing risk and reward, offering insights on how to calculate your tolerance for risk in the pursuit of financial freedom.

Understanding Risk

Risk is an inherent aspect of any business venture or investment opportunity. It encompasses the possibility of experiencing losses or failing to achieve expected returns. Different factors contribute to the level of risk associated with a particular endeavor, including market volatility, competition, regulatory changes, and economic conditions. Recognizing the types of risks and their potential impact is essential for informed decision-making.

Types of Risk

1. Market Risk: Market fluctuations can significantly affect the value of investments or the demand for products and services in a business.

2. Business Risk: Factors such as operational inefficiencies, competition, and changes in consumer preferences pose risks to the viability and profitability of a business.

3. Financial Risk: Relates to the use of debt or leverage to finance operations or investments, which amplifies the impact of market fluctuations on returns.

4. Regulatory Risk: Changes in laws and regulations can impact the operating environment and profitability of businesses across various industries.

5. Liquidity Risk: Refers to the ease with which assets can be converted into cash without significantly impacting their value, crucial for businesses and investors alike.

Assessing Your Risk Tolerance

Determining your risk tolerance involves introspection and a realistic evaluation of your financial situation, goals, and psychological disposition. Several factors influence an individual's risk tolerance, including:

1. Financial Objectives: Consider your short-term and long-term financial goals, such as wealth accumulation, retirement planning, or funding education expenses.

2. Time Horizon: Evaluate the length of time you intend to hold investments or operate a business. Longer time horizons may allow for greater tolerance of short-term fluctuations in value.

3. Financial Capacity: Assess your financial resources, including income, savings, and assets available for investment or business ventures.

4. Psychological Factors: Understand your comfort level with uncertainty, volatility, and the potential for financial loss. Emotions such as fear, greed, and overconfidence can influence decision-making.

Risk Tolerance Assessment Tools

Numerous tools and methodologies exist to help individuals assess their risk tolerance and investment preferences. These include risk tolerance questionnaires, investment policy statements, and scenario analysis techniques. While these tools provide valuable insights, it's essential to interpret the results in conjunction with personal circumstances and objectives.

Risk tolerance questionnaires are tools used by investors and financial advisors to assess an individual's or organization's willingness and capacity to tolerate investment risk based on factors such as financial goals, time horizon, and emotional temperament. *Investment policy statements* are formal documents that outline an investor's objectives, constraints, and guidelines for making investment decisions, providing a framework for aligning investment strategies with specific goals and risk preferences. *Scenario analysis techniques* involve evaluating potential future outcomes by simulating various scenarios or situations to assess their impact on investments, helping investors and analysts make informed decisions and manage risks effectively in uncertain environments.

Balancing Risk and Reward

Achieving financial freedom requires striking a balance between risk and reward that aligns with your tolerance level and objectives. While higher-risk investments or business ventures may offer the potential for greater returns, they also entail increased exposure to loss. Conversely, conservative strategies may offer stability but may not generate substantial wealth over time.

Diversification

Diversification is a fundamental risk management strategy that involves spreading investments across different asset classes, industries, and geographic regions. By diversifying your portfolio or business interests, you can reduce the impact of adverse events on overall performance. However, diversification does not guarantee against losses, especially during widespread market downturns.

Risk Management Strategies

Implementing effective risk management strategies is crucial to mitigate the impact of adverse events and safeguard your business interests. Some common risk management techniques include:

1. Diversification: Diversify your business ventures across different sectors, markets, or product lines to spread risk and maximize potential returns.

2. Risk Transfer: Utilize strategies such as insurance policies, contractual agreements, or partnerships to transfer specific risks to other parties who are better equipped to handle them.

3. Contingency Planning: Develop contingency plans and alternative courses of action to address unforeseen challenges, such as supply chain disruptions, regulatory changes, or economic downturns.

4. Cash Flow Management: Maintain sufficient cash reserves and establish effective cash flow management practices to ensure liquidity during periods of financial strain or unexpected expenses.

5. Talent Retention: Invest in employee training, retention programs, and succession planning to mitigate the risks associated with key personnel turnover and talent shortages. *Personnel turnover* refers to the rate at which employees leave a company or organization, typically measured over a specific period, such as annually or quarterly. It encompasses both voluntary departures (resignations or retirements) and involuntary separations (layoffs or terminations) and is often used as a key metric to assess workforce stability and organizational health.

By integrating these risk management strategies into your business ventures, you can enhance resilience, minimize vulnerabilities, and position your ventures for long-term success.

Periodic Review and Adjustment

Risk tolerance is not static and may evolve over time in response to changes in personal circumstances, market conditions, and economic factors. It's essential to periodically review your investment portfolio or business strategy to ensure alignment with your risk tolerance and financial goals. Rebalancing your portfolio or adjusting your business strategy may be necessary to maintain an optimal risk-reward profile.

Conclusion

Assessing your tolerance for risk is a critical step in navigating the complex landscape of entrepreneurship and investment. By understanding the types of risks, evaluating your risk tolerance, and implementing sound risk management strategies, you can make informed decisions that support your journey toward financial freedom. Remember that risk is inherent in any endeavor, but with prudent planning and disciplined execution, you can optimize your chances of success while safeguarding your financial interests.

Introduction

In the pursuit of financial freedom, one of the most crucial decisions an entrepreneur must make is selecting the right business model. The business model serves as the foundation upon which your enterprise stands, defining how you generate revenue, deliver value to customers, and sustain profitability over time. With a myriad of options available, each with its unique advantages and challenges, navigating the landscape of business models requires careful consideration and strategic planning.

Understanding Business Models

Before delving into specific business models, it's essential to grasp the fundamental concepts underlying them. At its core, a business model outlines the way a company creates, delivers, and captures value. It encompasses various elements, including revenue streams, cost structures, customer segments, and distribution channels. By designing an effective business model, entrepreneurs can align their resources and activities to achieve sustainable growth and profitability.

The Importance of Choosing the Right Structure

Selecting the appropriate business model is akin to laying the groundwork for a successful venture. A well-suited structure not only maximizes revenue potential but also enhances operational efficiency and facilitates scalability.

Moreover, it aligns with your goals, preferences, and market dynamics, enabling you to capitalize on emerging opportunities and navigate industry disruptions effectively. Therefore, entrepreneurs must assess their unique circumstances and evaluate different business models to determine the optimal fit for their endeavors.

Exploring Traditional Models

1. The Brick-and-Mortar Model: Historically prevalent, this model involves establishing physical storefronts or offices to interact with customers directly. While offering a tangible presence and personalized service, brick-and-mortar businesses face challenges such as high overhead costs and limited geographical reach. However, with the integration of online platforms and omnichannel strategies, traditional retailers can enhance their competitiveness and adapt to evolving consumer preferences.

Omnichannel strategies involve creating a seamless and integrated experience for customers across various channels, including physical stores, websites, mobile apps, social media platforms, and other touchpoints. This approach aims to provide a consistent and cohesive experience regardless of the channel or device used by customers, thereby enhancing customer satisfaction, loyalty, and engagement with the brand.

2. Franchise Model: Franchising offers entrepreneurs the opportunity to leverage established brands, proven processes, and ongoing support provided by franchisors. By acquiring franchise rights, individuals can replicate successful business models while benefiting from centralized marketing efforts and economies of scale. Despite the advantages, franchisees must adhere to

stringent regulations and pay royalties, limiting their autonomy and potential for innovation.

Embracing Digital Transformation

1. E-commerce Model: With the proliferation of the internet, e-commerce has revolutionized the way businesses engage with customers and conduct transactions. By operating online storefronts, entrepreneurs can reach a global audience, streamline operations, and leverage data analytics to enhance customer experiences. However, e-commerce ventures must contend with fierce competition, cybersecurity threats, and logistical complexities associated with fulfillment and delivery.

2. Subscription-based Model: This model entails offering products or services to customers on a recurring basis in exchange for subscription fees. Common in industries such as software, media, and healthcare, subscription-based businesses foster long-term customer relationships and generate predictable revenue streams. Nevertheless, sustaining subscriber loyalty requires continuous innovation, value-added features, and responsive customer support.

Pioneering Innovative Approaches

1. Platform Model: Platforms serve as intermediaries that facilitate interactions and transactions between users, suppliers, and third-party providers. By fostering network effects and enabling user-generated content, platforms such as Airbnb, Uber, and Amazon Marketplace have disrupted traditional industries and unlocked new revenue streams. However, platform businesses must address regulatory concerns, data privacy issues, and maintain trust among stakeholders to ensure sustainable growth.

2. Freemium Model: Popularized by software companies and digital services, the freemium model offers basic features or services for free while charging users for premium upgrades or advanced functionalities. By lowering entry barriers and encouraging user adoption, freemium businesses can expand their user base and monetize value-added offerings effectively. Nonetheless, striking a balance between free and paid tiers, and delivering compelling value propositions is essential to convert free users into paying customers.

Factors Influencing Business Model Selection

When evaluating different business models, several factors come into play, shaping your decision-making process.

1. Market Dynamics: Assessing market trends, competitive landscape, and consumer preferences helps identify viable opportunities and potential risks associated with specific business models.

2. Resource Allocation: Consideration of financial resources, human capital, and operational capabilities influences your ability to execute and sustain the chosen business model effectively.

3. Risk Appetite: Understanding your risk tolerance and resilience enables you to mitigate uncertainties and navigate challenges inherent in the chosen business model.

4. Scalability: Evaluating the scalability potential of different business models allows you to capitalize on growth opportunities and expand your market presence over time.

Conclusion

In the quest for financial freedom, selecting the right business model is paramount to long-term success and sustainability. By exploring different models, understanding their nuances, and aligning them with your objectives and resources, you can embark on a transformative journey towards entrepreneurial success. Remember, the journey of entrepreneurship is dynamic and evolving, requiring adaptability, resilience, and a willingness to embrace change. Armed with knowledge, foresight, and strategic insight, you can navigate the complexities of business model selection and chart a course towards prosperity and fulfillment.

Introduction

In the modern landscape of entrepreneurship, service-based businesses have emerged as a viable pathway towards financial freedom. Unlike traditional brick-and-mortar ventures, service-based businesses rely on the expertise, skills, and knowledge of individuals to offer solutions to clients' needs. In this article, we delve into the dynamics of service-based businesses, focusing on consulting, freelancing, and beyond.

The Rise of Service-Based Businesses

Service-based businesses have gained momentum in recent years due to several factors. The digital revolution has facilitated remote work and communication, enabling professionals to offer their services globally. Moreover, the gig economy and the increasing demand for specialized skills have created fertile ground for service-based entrepreneurs to thrive.

The *gig economy* refers to a labor market characterized by short-term and freelance work arrangements, often facilitated by digital platforms and technology. Workers in the gig economy typically perform tasks or "gigs" on a temporary or project basis, with flexibility in their schedules and the ability to work for multiple employers or clients simultaneously. This model contrasts with traditional full-time employment and is prevalent in sectors such as ride-sharing, food delivery, freelancing, and other on-demand services.

Consulting

Consulting is a form of service-based business where individuals or firms provide expert advice and guidance to clients seeking solutions to specific problems or challenges. Consultants leverage their knowledge, experience, and industry insights to offer tailored strategies and recommendations.

1. Specialization and Niche Expertise: Successful consultants often specialize in specific industries or areas of expertise, allowing them to position themselves as authorities in their respective fields.

2. Building Credibility and Trust: Establishing credibility and trust is paramount in the consulting industry. Consultants achieve this by delivering tangible results, maintaining integrity, and cultivating strong relationships with clients.

3. Value-Based Pricing: Unlike traditional businesses, consulting services are often priced based on the value they deliver rather than the time invested. This model incentivizes consultants to focus on outcomes and encourages clients to perceive the services as investments rather than expenses.

Freelancing

Freelancing has become a popular choice for individuals seeking autonomy and flexibility in their careers. Freelancers offer a wide range of services, from graphic design and writing to programming and digital marketing, catering to diverse client needs.

1. Remote Work and Digital Platforms: The proliferation of remote work opportunities and online freelancing platforms such as Upwork and Freelancer.com has democratized access to freelance opportunities. Freelancers can now collaborate with clients worldwide without geographical constraints.

2. Portfolio Careers: Many freelancers adopt a portfolio career approach, diversifying their skill sets and income streams across multiple projects and clients. This not only mitigates the risk of dependency on a single source of income but also fosters continuous learning and professional growth.

3. Challenges of Freelancing: Despite its appeal, freelancing comes with its own set of challenges, including inconsistent income, client management issues, and the need for self-discipline and time management. Successful freelancers proactively address these challenges by honing their communication skills, setting clear boundaries, and cultivating resilience.

Beyond Consulting and Freelancing

Beyond traditional consulting and freelancing, emerging service-based business models are redefining the landscape of entrepreneurship. From coaching and online courses to subscription-based services and digital agencies, entrepreneurs are experimenting with innovative approaches to delivering value and generating revenue.

1. Coaching and Mentorship: Coaching involves providing guidance, support, and accountability to individuals or

groups seeking personal or professional development. Coaches leverage their expertise and interpersonal skills to empower clients to achieve their goals and unlock their full potential.

2. Online Courses and Education: With the rise of e-learning platforms such as Udemy and Teachable, entrepreneurs can create and monetize online courses on a wide range of topics, from digital marketing and entrepreneurship to yoga and photography. Online courses offer scalability and passive income potential, allowing creators to reach a global audience and generate revenue while they sleep.

3. Subscription-Based Services: Subscription-based models have gained popularity across various industries, offering recurring revenue streams and fostering long-term customer relationships. From software as a service (SaaS) and content subscriptions to meal kits and beauty boxes, subscription-based businesses capitalize on convenience, personalization, and value delivery. Meal kits and beauty boxes are subscription-based services that deliver curated products to consumers on a regular basis.

Meal kits are packages containing pre-portioned ingredients and recipes for preparing meals at home. Subscribers receive a box containing all the necessary ingredients, often fresh and prepped, along with detailed cooking instructions. Meal kits offer convenience and variety to individuals and families looking to cook at home without the hassle of meal planning and grocery shopping.

Beauty boxes are subscription services that provide a selection of beauty and skincare products to customers on a recurring basis. These boxes typically contain samples or full-sized products from various brands, allowing subscribers to explore new products and trends in the beauty industry. Beauty boxes often cater to specific preferences such as skincare, makeup, haircare, or fragrance, offering a personalized experience to subscribers.

Conclusion

Service-based businesses offer a pathway towards financial freedom and fulfillment for aspiring entrepreneurs. Whether through consulting, freelancing, coaching, or innovative business models, individuals can leverage their skills, expertise, and passion to create value, impact lives, and achieve their entrepreneurial dreams. By understanding the dynamics, challenges, and opportunities of service-based businesses, entrepreneurs can navigate the journey towards success with clarity, resilience, and purpose.

Introduction

In the landscape of entrepreneurship, product-based businesses stand as pillars of innovation and commerce. From manufacturing to retail and e-commerce, the avenues for creating and distributing products are diverse and dynamic. In the pursuit of financial freedom, understanding the intricacies and opportunities within these sectors is paramount. This article delves into the world of product-based businesses, examining manufacturing, retail, and e-commerce as avenues for aspiring entrepreneurs.

Understanding Manufacturing Businesses

Manufacturing businesses form the backbone of many economies, contributing to job creation and economic growth. These enterprises involve the production of tangible goods, ranging from automobiles to consumer electronics and beyond. The manufacturing process encompasses various stages, including design, raw material acquisition, production, quality control, and distribution.

One of the key advantages of manufacturing businesses is the ability to exercise control over the entire production process. Entrepreneurs can innovate and customize products according to market demands, thereby establishing a competitive edge. However, manufacturing entails significant initial investment in infrastructure, machinery, and labor. Moreover, operational challenges such as supply chain disruptions and inventory management must be carefully navigated.

Despite these challenges, manufacturing businesses offer immense scalability and profit potential. By optimizing production processes and leveraging technological advancements, entrepreneurs can enhance efficiency and drive growth. Additionally, establishing strategic partnerships with suppliers and distributors can facilitate market penetration and expansion.

Navigating the Retail Landscape

Retail businesses play a pivotal role in connecting manufacturers with consumers, acting as intermediaries in the product distribution chain. From brick-and-mortar stores to online marketplaces, retailers cater to diverse consumer preferences and shopping behaviors. The retail sector encompasses a myriad of industries, including fashion, electronics, groceries, and specialty goods.

One of the defining features of retail businesses is the emphasis on customer experience and satisfaction. Successful retailers prioritize product presentation, pricing strategies, and personalized services to enhance customer engagement and loyalty. Furthermore, effective inventory management and supply chain logistics are essential for maintaining optimal stock levels and fulfilling customer demands.

In recent years, the rise of e-commerce has revolutionized the retail landscape, offering unprecedented convenience and accessibility to consumers worldwide. Online retailers leverage digital platforms and technologies to reach a global audience, transcending geographical boundaries and time constraints. However, the proliferation of e-commerce has intensified competition, necessitating innovative marketing tactics and omnichannel strategies.

Unleashing the Potential of E-Commerce Ventures

E-commerce has emerged as a disruptive force, reshaping traditional business models and redefining the dynamics of consumer engagement. From online marketplaces to direct-to-consumer brands, e-commerce ventures span a spectrum of industries and niches. The proliferation of smartphones and internet connectivity has fueled the exponential growth of online shopping, presenting lucrative opportunities for entrepreneurs.

One of the primary advantages of e-commerce ventures is the low barrier to entry compared to traditional retail channels. Entrepreneurs can launch online stores with minimal upfront investment, leveraging third-party platforms and digital marketing tools. Furthermore, e-commerce offers unparalleled flexibility and scalability, enabling businesses to adapt to evolving market trends and consumer preferences.

However, succeeding in the e-commerce landscape requires a comprehensive understanding of digital marketing strategies, search engine optimization (SEO), and customer relationship management (CRM). Building brand awareness and establishing trust are paramount in a crowded marketplace characterized by fierce competition and changing algorithms. Moreover, optimizing the user experience and streamlining checkout processes are critical for reducing cart abandonment rates and maximizing conversion rates.

Search Engine Optimization (SEO) is the process of optimizing a website's content, structure, and other elements to increase its visibility and ranking in search engine results pages (SERPs). SEO aims to attract organic (non-paid) traffic to a website by improving its relevance and authority for specific search queries, ultimately driving more visitors and potential customers.

Customer Relationship Management (CRM) refers to a set of strategies, practices, and technologies used by businesses to manage and analyze interactions with current and potential customers. CRM systems help organizations track customer interactions across various touchpoints, such as emails, phone calls, social media, and website visits, with the goal of improving customer retention, satisfaction, and loyalty.

Conclusion

Exploring product-based businesses entails a journey of innovation, resilience, and adaptation. Whether in manufacturing, retail, or e-commerce, entrepreneurs must navigate dynamic market forces and capitalize on emerging opportunities. By understanding the unique challenges and nuances within each sector, aspiring business owners can make informed decisions and chart a path towards financial freedom.

Manufacturing businesses offer the potential for customization and scale, albeit with substantial initial investment and operational complexities. Retail enterprises thrive on customer-centricity and omnichannel strategies, bridging the gap between manufacturers and consumers. E-commerce ventures empower entrepreneurs to harness the power of digital platforms and global connectivity, albeit amidst intensifying competition and evolving consumer expectations.

In the pursuit of financial freedom, embracing innovation and adaptation are paramount. As technology continues to reshape the business landscape, entrepreneurs must remain agile and responsive to changing market dynamics. By leveraging creativity, resilience, and strategic foresight, aspiring business owners can embark on a transformative journey towards entrepreneurial success in the realm of product-based businesses.

Introduction

In today's fast-paced business landscape, staying ahead requires more than just keeping up with the latest trends. It demands a proactive approach to leveraging technology and innovation to drive growth and maintain relevance. As businesses navigate the complexities of a digital world, understanding how to harness the power of technology becomes paramount. This article explores the importance of leveraging technology and innovation and provides insights into how businesses can stay ahead in an increasingly digital environment.

Embracing Digital Transformation

The rapid evolution of technology has transformed the way businesses operate. From artificial intelligence and machine learning to blockchain and the Internet of Things (IoT), the digital landscape offers a plethora of opportunities for innovation. Embracing digital transformation is no longer optional; it's a necessity for survival in today's competitive market.

Artificial intelligence (AI) refers to the simulation of human intelligence processes by machines, including learning, reasoning, and problem-solving. *Machine learning* is a subset of artificial intelligence that enables systems to automatically learn and improve from experience without being explicitly programmed, often through the use of algorithms and statistical models.

Blockchain is a decentralized and distributed digital ledger technology that records transactions across multiple computers in a way that is transparent, secure, and tamper-resistant. The *Internet of Things* (IoT) refers to the network of interconnected devices, sensors, and objects that communicate and exchange data with each other over the internet, enabling real-time monitoring, control, and automation of physical processes.

Businesses must adopt a forward-thinking mindset and embrace digital technologies to streamline processes, enhance efficiency, and improve customer experiences. By leveraging automation and data analytics, organizations can gain valuable insights into consumer behavior, optimize operations, and make informed decisions.

Fostering a Culture of Innovation

Innovation lies at the heart of every successful business. Fostering a culture of innovation encourages creativity, collaboration, and continuous improvement. In a digital world where change is constant, businesses must prioritize innovation to stay ahead of the curve.

Encouraging employees to think outside the box, experiment with new ideas, and embrace failure as a learning opportunity fosters a culture of innovation. By empowering employees to contribute their unique perspectives and insights, businesses can unlock untapped potential and drive meaningful change.

Leveraging Data Analytics for Strategic Insights

Data has emerged as a valuable asset in today's digital economy. From customer preferences and market trends to operational efficiency and performance metrics, data analytics provides businesses with valuable insights to drive strategic decision-making.

By leveraging advanced analytics tools and techniques, businesses can uncover patterns, identify opportunities, and mitigate risks. Whether it's predicting consumer behavior, optimizing supply chain management, or personalizing marketing campaigns, data analytics enables businesses to make data-driven decisions that drive growth and innovation.

Embracing Artificial Intelligence and Machine Learning

Artificial intelligence (AI) and machine learning (ML) are revolutionizing the way businesses operate. From chatbots and virtual assistants to predictive analytics and automation, AI and ML technologies offer a myriad of opportunities to enhance efficiency and drive innovation.

Chatbots are computer programs designed to simulate human conversation through text or voice interactions, often used for customer service, information retrieval, or task automation. *Virtual assistants* are software-based agents or applications that provide assistance to users through natural language processing and voice recognition, helping with tasks such as scheduling, reminders, information retrieval, and automation. *Predictive analytics* involves the use of statistical algorithms and machine learning techniques to analyze historical data and predict future outcomes or trends, enabling businesses to make informed decisions and take proactive actions. *Automation* refers to the use of technology to perform tasks or processes with minimal human intervention, streamlining workflows, reducing errors, and improving efficiency across various industries and functions.

By automating repetitive tasks and processes, businesses can free up valuable time and resources to focus on higher-value activities. AI-powered algorithms can analyze vast amounts of data in real-time, enabling businesses to uncover insights and make proactive decisions.

Harnessing the Power of Blockchain Technology

Blockchain technology has gained widespread attention for its potential to revolutionize industries ranging from finance and healthcare to supply chain management and beyond. By providing a secure, transparent, and immutable ledger of transactions, blockchain technology offers a decentralized approach to data management and authentication.

Businesses can leverage blockchain technology to streamline processes, reduce costs, and mitigate risks. Whether it's facilitating secure transactions, tracking the provenance of goods, or ensuring data integrity, blockchain technology offers a myriad of opportunities for innovation and disruption.

Adapting to Evolving Consumer Trends

In today's digital world, consumer preferences are constantly evolving. From the rise of e-commerce and mobile shopping to the increasing demand for personalized experiences and instant gratification, businesses must adapt to meet the changing needs and expectations of their customers.

By leveraging technology and innovation, businesses can anticipate consumer trends, personalize offerings, and deliver seamless experiences across channels. Whether it's implementing omnichannel strategies, embracing mobile payment solutions, or harnessing the power of social media, businesses must stay agile and responsive to remain competitive in today's digital marketplace.

Investing in Talent and Skills Development

In a digital world where technology is constantly evolving, investing in talent and skills development is essential for staying ahead. Businesses must prioritize employee training and development to ensure that their teams have the knowledge and expertise needed to leverage emerging technologies and drive innovation.

From technical skills such as coding and data analysis to soft skills such as creativity and problem-solving, businesses must equip their employees with the tools and resources they need to thrive in a digital environment. By investing in talent development, businesses can build a skilled workforce that is capable of driving growth and innovation in an increasingly digital world.

Conclusion

Leveraging technology and innovation is essential for staying ahead in today's digital world. By embracing digital transformation, fostering a culture of innovation, and leveraging advanced technologies such as data analytics, artificial intelligence, and blockchain, businesses can unlock new opportunities for growth and differentiation.

Adapting to evolving consumer trends, investing in talent and skills development, and embracing a forward-thinking mindset are also critical for success in today's fast-paced business landscape. By staying agile, responsive, and committed to innovation, businesses can position themselves for long-term success and financial freedom in an increasingly digital world.

Introduction

In the dynamic landscape of entrepreneurship, funding your venture stands as one of the pivotal steps towards realizing your business aspirations. Whether you're launching a startup or expanding an existing enterprise, navigating the diverse array of financing options and strategies is crucial for sustainable growth and success. This article delves into the multifaceted realm of funding, offering insights into various avenues and strategies tailored to empower entrepreneurs on their journey towards financial freedom.

Understanding Financing Options

Before delving into specific strategies, it's essential to grasp the spectrum of financing options available to entrepreneurs. From traditional bank loans to cutting-edge crowdfunding platforms, each avenue presents unique advantages and challenges.

1. Traditional Bank Loans

Traditional bank loans remain a cornerstone of financing for many entrepreneurs. These loans typically offer competitive interest rates and structured repayment plans, making them an attractive option for established businesses with solid credit histories. However, securing a bank loan often requires a rigorous application process, including detailed financial documentation and collateral.

2. Venture Capital

Venture capital is a type of private equity financing provided to early-stage or high-growth companies in exchange for equity ownership, typically by institutional investors or investment firms. For high-growth startups with ambitious visions, venture capital presents a compelling funding avenue. Venture capital firms inject capital into promising ventures in exchange for equity stakes, providing not only financial support but also strategic guidance and industry connections. While venture capital can fuel rapid expansion, entrepreneurs must be prepared to cede partial ownership and adhere to stringent growth targets set by investors.

3. Angel Investors

Angel investors, often affluent individuals seeking high-potential investment opportunities, play a pivotal role in financing early-stage startups. Unlike venture capital firms, angel investors typically invest their personal funds, offering entrepreneurs greater flexibility and autonomy. Building relationships with angel investors requires effective networking and pitching skills, as securing funding often hinges on personal rapport and shared vision.

4. Crowdfunding

Crowdfunding is a method of raising capital for a project or venture by soliciting small contributions from a large number of people, typically via online platforms. In recent years, crowdfunding platforms have emerged as a democratized alternative to traditional financing channels. Through platforms like Kickstarter and Indiegogo, entrepreneurs can showcase their projects to a global audience and solicit financial contributions in exchange for rewards or equity. Crowdfunding empowers entrepreneurs to validate their ideas, engage with prospective customers, and generate buzz while bypassing traditional gatekeepers.

Crafting a Financing Strategy

In crafting a financing strategy tailored to your venture's unique needs and aspirations, it's essential to adopt a holistic approach that balances short-term capital requirements with long-term growth objectives. Consider the following guiding principles.

1. Assessing Financial Needs

Before embarking on your fundraising journey, conduct a comprehensive assessment of your venture's financial needs across various stages of growth. Evaluate factors such as startup costs, operational expenses, expansion plans, and contingencies to determine the optimal funding amount and timeline.

2. Diversifying Funding Sources

Diversification is key to mitigating risk and maximizing financial resilience. Rather than relying solely on a single financing source, explore opportunities to diversify your funding portfolio across multiple channels. By blending traditional loans with equity investments, grants, and revenue streams, you can create a robust financial foundation capable of weathering economic uncertainties.

Equity investments involve securing capital for business ventures by selling shares or ownership stakes in the company to investors in exchange for funding, allowing investors to participate in the company's growth and success. *Grants* are non-repayable funds provided by governments, organizations, or institutions to support specific business ventures or initiatives, offering a source of financing that does not require repayment, typically based on meeting certain criteria or objectives. *Revenue streams* represent the various sources of income generated by a business venture through sales, services, subscriptions, or other revenue-generating activities, providing ongoing financial support and sustainability for the venture.

3. Building Strategic Partnerships

Beyond financial capital, strategic partnerships can unlock a wealth of resources, expertise, and market opportunities for your venture. Cultivate relationships with industry stakeholders, corporate sponsors, and strategic investors who share your vision and can contribute value beyond monetary support. Collaborative partnerships can accelerate growth, enhance credibility, and open doors to new markets and distribution channels.

4. Embracing Bootstrapping

Bootstrapping refers to the practice of financing a business venture with personal savings, revenue generated by the business, or other non-traditional methods, such as borrowing from friends and family, instead of relying on external funding sources like venture capital or bank loans. While external funding can provide essential fuel for growth, don't overlook the power of bootstrapping – the practice of self-funding your venture through personal savings, revenue reinvestment, and cost-effective strategies. Bootstrapping instills discipline, resourcefulness, and a relentless focus on profitability, enabling entrepreneurs to maintain autonomy and preserve equity while navigating the unpredictable terrain of entrepreneurship.

Navigating Challenges and Pitfalls

Despite the abundance of financing options, navigating the funding landscape is fraught with challenges and pitfalls. From stringent eligibility criteria to market fluctuations and investor skepticism, entrepreneurs must be prepared to confront and overcome obstacles on their path to financial freedom.

1. Managing Investor Expectations

When engaging with investors, transparency, and integrity are paramount. Clearly communicate your business model, growth projections, and risk factors, setting realistic expectations regarding returns and timelines. Establishing open lines of communication and fostering trust is essential for building enduring investor relationships based on mutual respect and alignment of interests.

2. Mitigating Financial Risks

Financial prudence is the cornerstone of sustainable entrepreneurship. Conduct thorough due diligence, assess potential risks, and develop contingency plans to mitigate financial vulnerabilities and safeguard against unforeseen challenges. Adopt a conservative approach to financial management, prioritizing cash flow stability, and preserving liquidity to weather downturns and capitalize on emerging opportunities.

3. Adapting to Market Dynamics

In a rapidly evolving business landscape, adaptability is the key to resilience. Stay attuned to market trends, consumer preferences, and competitive dynamics, iterating your business model and financing strategy in response to changing external forces. Embrace agility, experimentation, and continuous learning as core principles guiding your entrepreneurial journey.

Conclusion

Funding your venture is not merely a financial transaction but a strategic imperative that shapes the trajectory of your entrepreneurial endeavor. By understanding the diverse array of financing options, crafting a resilient financing strategy, and navigating challenges with agility and foresight, entrepreneurs can position themselves for sustained growth, innovation, and ultimately, financial freedom. As you embark on your entrepreneurial odyssey, remember that while the path may be fraught with uncertainties and obstacles, it is also adorned with boundless opportunities for those bold enough to seize them.

Introduction

In the dynamic landscape of business, navigating legal and regulatory requirements stands as a critical pillar for sustainable growth and success. Whether you're a seasoned entrepreneur or a budding startup, understanding the nuances of compliance is indispensable. This article delves into the intricacies of compliance and explores its significance beyond mere adherence to laws and regulations.

The Foundation of Compliance

Compliance forms the cornerstone of every business endeavor. At its essence, compliance refers to the alignment of business practices with applicable laws, regulations, and standards. It encompasses various aspects, including financial regulations, data protection laws, employment laws, environmental regulations, and industry-specific mandates. Establishing a robust compliance framework not only mitigates legal risks but also fosters trust among stakeholders.

The Regulatory Landscape

The regulatory landscape is multifaceted and continually evolving. Businesses operate within a framework governed by federal, state, and local regulations, along with industry-specific guidelines. From tax laws to consumer protection regulations, the scope of compliance extends across diverse domains. Staying abreast of regulatory updates and amendments is imperative to ensure adherence and avoid potential penalties or legal repercussions.

Compliance as a Competitive Advantage

Beyond regulatory mandates, compliance can serve as a catalyst for competitiveness and differentiation. Proactively embracing ethical standards and best practices enhances corporate reputation and credibility. In an era characterized by heightened scrutiny and transparency, consumers and investors gravitate towards businesses with a demonstrable commitment to compliance and corporate responsibility. Moreover, adherence to quality standards and regulatory benchmarks instills confidence in the product or service offerings, fostering long-term customer loyalty.

The Evolving Regulatory Landscape

The business environment is subject to constant regulatory flux, presenting both challenges and opportunities. Regulatory changes may necessitate adjustments to operational processes, resource allocation, and strategic planning. Flexibility and adaptability emerge as indispensable traits in navigating regulatory uncertainties. Moreover, proactive engagement with regulatory bodies and industry associations enables businesses to influence policy formulation and advocate for favorable outcomes.

Compliance Beyond Borders

In an interconnected global economy, businesses encounter regulatory complexities transcending geographical boundaries. International trade agreements, cross-border transactions, and foreign investment regulations add layers of intricacy to compliance management. Operating across jurisdictions requires a nuanced understanding of legal frameworks, cultural nuances, and geopolitical dynamics. Collaboration with legal experts and consultants versed in international law facilitates seamless expansion into new markets while mitigating compliance risks.

Embracing Ethical Governance

Compliance extends beyond regulatory mandates to encompass ethical governance and corporate stewardship. Upholding ethical principles and values forms the bedrock of organizational integrity. Ethical lapses not only tarnish reputation but also erode stakeholder trust and confidence. Embedding a culture of ethics and accountability fosters a conducive work environment and cultivates a sense of shared purpose among employees. Ethical governance transcends compliance requirements, serving as a guiding beacon for responsible decision-making and sustainable business practices.

Leveraging Technology for Compliance Management

In an era characterized by digital transformation, technology emerges as a potent enabler for compliance management. Innovative solutions leveraging artificial intelligence, data analytics, and automation streamline compliance workflows, enhance risk detection capabilities, and facilitate real-time monitoring. Cloud-based platforms and software-as-a-service (SaaS) offerings offer scalable and cost-effective solutions tailored to diverse business needs. Embracing technology-driven compliance tools empowers businesses to proactively identify emerging risks and preemptively address compliance gaps.

The Role of Leadership in Compliance Culture

Leadership plays a pivotal role in shaping organizational culture and fostering a commitment to compliance excellence. From the executive suite to frontline managers, leaders set the tone for ethical conduct and regulatory compliance. By championing a culture of transparency, accountability, and continuous improvement, leaders inspire employee buy-in and collective ownership of compliance objectives. Moreover, effective communication channels and training programs ensure that employees are equipped with the knowledge and resources to uphold compliance standards in their day-to-day activities.

Conclusion

Navigating legal and regulatory requirements is an indispensable facet of modern business operations. Compliance transcends mere adherence to laws and regulations; it embodies a commitment to ethical governance, corporate responsibility, and stakeholder trust. As businesses navigate the complex regulatory landscape, embracing compliance as a strategic imperative unlocks opportunities for sustainable growth, competitive differentiation, and enduring success. By fostering a culture of compliance excellence and leveraging technology-driven solutions, businesses can navigate regulatory challenges with confidence and chart a course towards financial freedom and prosperity.

Introduction

In the dynamic landscape of entrepreneurship, the adage "no man is an island" rings truer than ever. Every successful business venture is a testament to the power of collaboration and the strength of a cohesive team. As entrepreneurs, one of the most crucial decisions we make is choosing the individuals who will join us on our journey towards success. Building a strong team is not just about finding people to fill roles; it's about surrounding yourself with the right individuals who share your vision, complement your skills, and propel your business forward.

Understanding the Importance of Team Building

The foundation of any successful business lies in its team. A cohesive and high-functioning team can achieve far more than the sum of its parts. Team building is not just about assembling a group of individuals with impressive resumes; it's about creating a synergy where each member contributes their unique talents and perspectives towards a common goal.

Identifying Your Core Values and Vision

Before you begin assembling your team, it's essential to have a clear understanding of your core values and vision for your business. Your values serve as the guiding principles that will shape your company culture and define the type of individuals you want to attract. When your team shares these values, it fosters a sense of alignment and cohesion, making it easier to work towards shared objectives.

Recruitment Strategies for Finding the Right Talent

Recruiting the right talent is both an art and a science. It requires a strategic approach that goes beyond simply evaluating resumes and qualifications. Look for individuals who not only possess the necessary skills and experience but also demonstrate a genuine passion for your industry and a commitment to your vision.

Cultural Fit and Team Dynamics

Cultural fit is often cited as one of the most critical factors in team building. While skills and experience are undoubtedly important, they should not overshadow the importance of cultural alignment. A team that shares common values, communicates effectively, and respects each other's contributions is better equipped to overcome challenges and achieve collective success.

Fostering Communication and Collaboration

Effective communication lies at the heart of every successful team. Encourage open dialogue, active listening, and constructive feedback among team members. Foster an environment where ideas are valued, and everyone feels empowered to contribute their insights and perspectives. Collaboration thrives in an atmosphere of trust and mutual respect, so prioritize building strong interpersonal relationships within your team.

Embracing Diversity and Inclusion

Diversity is not just a buzzword; it's a strategic imperative for building a strong and resilient team. Embrace diversity in all its forms – whether it's cultural, ethnic, gender, or experiential. A diverse team brings a wealth of perspectives and ideas to the table, driving innovation and creativity. Inclusion is equally important; ensure that every team member feels valued, respected, and empowered to thrive.

Empowering Your Team for Success

As a leader, your role is not only to delegate tasks but to empower your team members to reach their full potential. Provide them with the resources, support, and guidance they need to excel in their roles. Encourage autonomy and initiative, allowing team members to take ownership of their projects and contribute meaningfully to the organization's success.

Nurturing a Culture of Continuous Learning and Growth

The business landscape is constantly evolving, and successful teams are those that embrace change and adaptability. Foster a culture of continuous learning and growth within your team, encouraging members to seek out new skills, knowledge, and experiences. Invest in training and development opportunities that enable your team to stay ahead of the curve and remain competitive in a rapidly changing world.

Celebrating Achievements and Recognizing Contributions

Acknowledging the contributions and achievements of your team members is crucial for morale and motivation. Celebrate milestones, both big and small, and recognize individuals for their hard work, dedication, and accomplishments. A culture of appreciation and recognition fosters loyalty and commitment, inspiring team members to continue striving for excellence.

Navigating Challenges and Resolving Conflicts

No team is immune to challenges and conflicts, but how they are addressed can make all the difference. Encourage open and honest dialogue when conflicts arise, and work collaboratively towards finding solutions that benefit everyone involved. Foster a culture of accountability and responsibility, where team members take ownership of their actions and work towards collective resolutions.

Conclusion

Building a strong team is not just about finding the right people; it's about cultivating a culture of collaboration, communication, and shared purpose. By surrounding yourself with individuals who share your values, complement your skills, and embrace diversity, you lay the foundation for success in any business venture. Remember, your team is not just a collection of individuals – it's the driving force behind your journey towards financial freedom and entrepreneurial success.

Introduction

In today's competitive business landscape, building a strong brand presence and effective marketing strategies are essential for success. Whether you're launching a startup or managing an established business, your brand identity and marketing efforts play a significant role in attracting customers, driving sales, and fostering long-term growth. This article explores key concepts and strategies to help businesses establish a robust brand presence and execute effective marketing campaigns.

Understanding Branding

Branding encompasses more than just a logo or a catchy slogan; it represents the overall perception and reputation of your business in the minds of consumers. Successful branding creates a unique identity that distinguishes your products or services from competitors and resonates with your target audience. It's about conveying your values, mission, and promises consistently across all touchpoints, including your website, social media channels, packaging, and customer interactions.

Defining Your Brand Identity

Before implementing any marketing strategies, it's crucial to define your brand identity. Start by clarifying your mission, values, and what sets your business apart from others. Consider your target audience demographics, preferences, and pain points to tailor your brand messaging effectively. Your brand identity should reflect authenticity, relevance, and credibility to establish trust and emotional connections with consumers.

Crafting Compelling Brand Messaging

Effective brand messaging communicates the essence of your brand and resonates with your target audience. Develop a clear and concise brand story that articulates who you are, what you offer, and why it matters. Your messaging should address consumer needs, evoke emotions, and showcase the value proposition of your products or services. Use language and visuals that align with your brand personality and evoke the desired perceptions and emotions among consumers.

Building Brand Consistency

Consistency is key to building a strong brand presence and fostering brand recognition. Ensure that your branding elements, including logos, colors, fonts, and imagery, are cohesive and consistently applied across all marketing channels and platforms. Consistent branding reinforces brand recall and helps consumers associate your business with positive experiences and values. Implement brand guidelines to maintain consistency and coherence in all brand communications and visual assets.

Leveraging Digital Marketing Channels

In today's digital age, leveraging online channels is essential for reaching and engaging with your target audience effectively. Develop a comprehensive digital marketing strategy that encompasses various platforms such as social media, search engines, email marketing, and content marketing. Identify the channels where your target audience is most active and tailor your messaging and content to resonate with their preferences and interests.

Harnessing the Power of Social Media

Social media platforms offer invaluable opportunities to build brand awareness, engage with customers, and drive conversions. Establish a strong presence on relevant social media channels such as Facebook, Instagram, Twitter, LinkedIn, and TikTok, based on your target audience demographics and behavior. Create compelling content that entertains, educates, or inspires your audience while staying true to your brand voice and values. Encourage user-generated content and foster meaningful interactions to cultivate a loyal community of brand advocates.

Optimizing Search Engine Visibility

Search engine optimization (SEO) plays a critical role in improving your website's visibility and driving organic traffic. Conduct keyword research to identify relevant search terms and phrases used by your target audience. Optimize your website content, meta tags, and backlink profile to enhance your search engine rankings and increase your online visibility. Regularly monitor and analyze your SEO performance metrics to identify areas for improvement and refine your optimization strategies accordingly.

Embracing Content Marketing

Content marketing involves creating and distributing valuable, relevant, and engaging content to attract and retain your target audience. Develop a content strategy that aligns with your brand objectives and addresses the needs and interests of your target audience. Create diverse content formats such as blog posts, articles, videos, infographics, podcasts, and eBooks to cater to different preferences and consumption habits. Share your expertise, insights, and storytelling to establish thought leadership and build credibility within your industry.

Infographics are visual representations of information, data, or knowledge designed to present complex concepts or data in a clear, concise, and engaging format, typically combining text, images, and graphical elements to communicate key messages effectively. *Podcasts* are digital audio or video files that are episodic in nature and available for streaming or download over the internet. Podcasts cover a wide range of topics and formats, including interviews, storytelling, discussions, and educational content, providing listeners with on-demand access to engaging and informative audio content.

Engaging Influencers and Partnerships

Collaborating with influencers, industry experts, and strategic partners can amplify your brand reach and credibility. Identify influencers and partners whose values, audience, and expertise align with your brand goals and target demographics. Forge authentic relationships and collaborations that provide mutual value and resonate with your audience's interests and aspirations. Leverage influencer marketing campaigns, co-branded initiatives, and affiliate partnerships to extend your brand's reach and foster trust among consumers.

Measuring and Optimizing Performance

Effective marketing strategies require ongoing monitoring, measurement, and optimization to ensure their effectiveness and return on investment (ROI). Utilize analytics tools and metrics to track key performance indicators (KPIs) such as website traffic, conversion rates, engagement metrics, and customer acquisition costs. *Conversion rates* indicate the proportion of users taking a desired action compared to the total number of visitors. *Engagement metrics* measure user interaction and involvement with a website, app, or content. *Customer acquisition costs* represent the total expenses incurred to acquire a new customer divided by the number of new customers gained.

Analyze data insights to identify trends, patterns, and areas for improvement in your branding and marketing efforts. Continuously iterate and optimize your strategies based on performance data and customer feedback to drive better results and achieve your business objectives.

Conclusion

Building a strong brand presence and executing effective marketing strategies are essential components of business success in today's competitive marketplace. By defining your brand identity, crafting compelling messaging, leveraging digital channels, and measuring performance, you can create meaningful connections with your target audience, drive engagement, and ultimately achieve sustainable growth and financial freedom for your business.

Introduction

In the realm of modern business, where competition is fierce and customer expectations are continually evolving, maintaining strong relationships with your clientele is paramount. Customer Relationship Management (CRM) stands as a cornerstone strategy for businesses striving not only to attract but also to retain loyal customers. In the pursuit of financial freedom, understanding the nuances of CRM and its role in fostering loyalty and satisfaction is essential.

Understanding Customer Relationship Management

At its core, Customer Relationship Management entails a comprehensive approach to managing interactions and relationships with both current and potential customers. It involves leveraging technology, data, and customer insights to personalize interactions, streamline processes, and ultimately enhance customer satisfaction. CRM systems serve as the backbone of this strategy, providing businesses with tools to effectively track, analyze, and respond to customer interactions across various touchpoints.

Building Trust and Engagement

Trust forms the bedrock of any successful customer relationship. In today's hyperconnected world, where consumers have access to an abundance of choices, earning and maintaining trust is non-negotiable. CRM enables businesses to cultivate trust by delivering consistent and personalized experiences tailored to individual preferences and needs. Through targeted communication, timely support, and proactive engagement, businesses can establish rapport and foster long-term loyalty.

Personalization

Personalization lies at the heart of effective CRM strategies. By harnessing the power of data analytics and segmentation, businesses can tailor their offerings and communications to resonate with each customer on a personal level. Whether through personalized recommendations, targeted promotions, or customized experiences, personalization demonstrates a deep understanding of the customer's preferences and drives higher levels of satisfaction and loyalty.

Effective Communication and Feedback Management

Communication serves as a linchpin in nurturing customer relationships. CRM systems enable businesses to streamline communication channels, ensuring timely responses and seamless interactions across multiple touchpoints. Furthermore, robust feedback management mechanisms empower businesses to solicit, analyze, and act upon customer feedback effectively. By listening attentively to customer concerns and addressing them promptly, businesses can instill confidence and demonstrate their commitment to customer satisfaction.

Anticipating and Addressing Customer Needs

Successful businesses go beyond merely reacting to customer needs; they anticipate them. Through predictive analytics and behavioral insights, CRM systems empower businesses to anticipate customer preferences, identify emerging trends, and proactively address evolving needs. By staying one step ahead, businesses can delight customers with relevant offerings and personalized solutions, fostering a sense of loyalty and satisfaction.

Creating Seamless Omni-Channel Experiences

In today's omnichannel landscape, where customers interact with brands across multiple platforms and devices, delivering seamless experiences is paramount. CRM facilitates the integration of disparate channels, allowing businesses to maintain a cohesive presence and deliver consistent messaging across all touchpoints. Whether through online platforms, mobile apps, social media, or traditional channels, businesses can ensure that every interaction contributes to a unified and compelling customer experience.

Leveraging Data for Actionable Insights

Data serves as the lifeblood of effective CRM strategies. By capturing and analyzing customer data at every touchpoint, businesses gain valuable insights into customer behavior, preferences, and pain points. These insights, in turn, inform strategic decision-making, enabling businesses to optimize their products, services, and marketing efforts for maximum impact. From identifying high-value customers to predicting churn risk, data-driven CRM empowers businesses to make informed decisions that drive loyalty and satisfaction. *Churn risk* refers to the likelihood that customers will discontinue or cancel their subscription, contract, or relationship with a business, often resulting in lost revenue and the need for retention strategies.

The Role of Customer Support and Service

Exceptional customer support is a cornerstone of effective CRM. Beyond resolving issues and addressing concerns, customer support serves as a critical touchpoint for building relationships and fostering trust. CRM systems facilitate the seamless management of customer inquiries, ensuring prompt resolution and personalized assistance. Moreover, by leveraging automation and self-service options, businesses can empower customers to find answers and resolve issues independently, enhancing satisfaction and reducing friction in the customer journey.

Measuring Success and Driving Continuous Improvement

In the pursuit of financial freedom, measuring the effectiveness of CRM initiatives is essential. Key performance indicators (KPIs) such as customer retention rates, customer lifetime value, and Net Promoter Score (NPS) provide valuable insights into the health of customer relationships and the overall impact of CRM efforts. *Customer retention rates* reflect the percentage of customers retained over a defined period, indicating business loyalty and satisfaction. *Customer lifetime value* quantifies the net profit anticipated from a customer throughout their relationship with a business, guiding strategic decisions on customer acquisition and retention. *Net Promoter Score* (NPS) assesses customer satisfaction and loyalty by gauging their likelihood to recommend a product or service to others, providing insights into overall customer sentiment.

By tracking these metrics and analyzing performance trends, businesses can identify areas for improvement and refine their CRM strategies iteratively. Continuous learning and adaptation are central to success in the ever-evolving landscape of customer relationship management.

Conclusion

In an era defined by rapid technological advancements and shifting consumer preferences, the significance of Customer Relationship Management cannot be overstated. By prioritizing trust, personalization, effective communication, and data-driven insights, businesses can cultivate lasting relationships with their customers, driving loyalty, satisfaction, and ultimately, financial freedom. Embracing CRM as a strategic imperative, businesses can navigate the complexities of the modern marketplace with confidence, unlocking new opportunities for growth and prosperity.

Introduction

In the dynamic landscape of business, financial management plays a pivotal role in the success and sustainability of any enterprise. This article will delve into the essential aspects of financial management, focusing on budgeting, forecasting, and cash flow. These pillars form the foundation for sound financial decisions, enabling businesses to thrive in a competitive environment.

Understanding Financial Management

Financial management involves planning, organizing, directing, and controlling an organization's financial resources. It encompasses a wide range of activities, from setting financial goals to implementing strategies that ensure optimal use of resources. A key component of financial management is the careful analysis and monitoring of various financial aspects, including budgeting, forecasting, and managing cash flow.

Budgeting

1. Definition and Purpose

Budgeting is the process of creating a detailed financial plan that outlines an organization's expected income and expenses over a specific period. The primary purpose of budgeting is to allocate resources efficiently, set financial goals, and provide a framework for evaluating performance.

2. Creating a Budget

To create an effective budget, businesses must consider historical financial data, market trends, and future growth projections. It involves estimating revenues, forecasting expenses, and aligning financial goals with the overall business strategy.

3. Types of Budgets

Operating Budget: Focuses on day-to-day expenses and income, including sales, production costs, and administrative expenses.

Capital Budget: Addresses long-term investments, such as purchasing equipment or expanding facilities.

Cash Flow Budget: Predicts cash inflows and outflows to ensure there's enough liquidity to cover operational needs.

4. Benefits of Budgeting

Budgeting offers several advantages, including improved financial discipline, enhanced decision-making, and the ability to identify potential issues before they become critical. It serves as a roadmap for financial success, guiding businesses toward their goals.

Forecasting

1. Definition and Significance

Forecasting involves predicting future trends based on historical data and market analysis. Businesses use forecasting to anticipate changes in the economic environment, consumer behavior, and industry trends, allowing them to make informed decisions.

2. Methods of Forecasting

Quantitative Methods: Utilize statistical models and historical data to predict future trends, such as time series analysis and regression analysis.

Qualitative Methods: Rely on expert opinions, market research, and subjective judgment to make predictions.

Combination Methods: Integrate both quantitative and qualitative approaches for a more comprehensive outlook.

3. Importance of Forecasting

Forecasting enables businesses to adapt to changing circumstances, identify potential opportunities, and mitigate risks. It aids in strategic planning, resource allocation, and maintaining a competitive edge in the market.

Cash Flow Management

1. Definition and Purpose

Cash flow management involves monitoring and controlling the movement of cash into and out of a business. It ensures that an organization has enough liquidity to cover its operational expenses while maintaining stability and growth.

2. Components of Cash Flow

Operating Activities: Inflows and outflows related to day-to-day business operations, such as sales and expenses.

Investing Activities: Involves cash transactions for long-term assets, such as buying or selling equipment.

Financing Activities: Includes cash transactions with investors and creditors, like issuing or repurchasing stock.

3. Strategies for Effective Cash Flow Management

Monitoring Receivables: Timely collection of accounts receivable to maintain a healthy cash flow.

Managing Payables: Negotiating favorable terms with suppliers to optimize cash flow.

Contingency Planning: Developing strategies to address unexpected disruptions that may impact cash flow.

4. Benefits of Efficient Cash Flow Management

A well-managed cash flow provides the financial flexibility necessary for seizing opportunities, weathering economic downturns, and ensuring the smooth operation of day-to-day activities.

Integrating Financial Management for Success

1. The Interconnectedness of Budgeting, Forecasting, and Cash Flow

These three elements of financial management are interconnected and complementary. A well-constructed budget serves as the foundation for forecasting, while accurate forecasts inform budget adjustments. Both budgeting and forecasting contribute to effective cash flow management, ensuring the financial health of the business.

2. Technology's Role in Financial Management

Advancements in technology have revolutionized financial management practices. Automation tools, financial software, and data analytics enable businesses to streamline budgeting, enhance forecasting accuracy, and improve cash flow visibility.

3. The Human Element in Financial Management

While technology plays a crucial role, the human element remains paramount in financial management. Skilled financial professionals who can interpret data, make strategic decisions, and adapt to evolving market conditions are indispensable for effective financial management.

Conclusion

Financial management is the cornerstone of a successful and sustainable business. By understanding and implementing sound budgeting, forecasting, and cash flow management practices, businesses can navigate the complexities of the modern economic landscape. Aspiring entrepreneurs seeking financial freedom should prioritize mastering these essential elements to build a resilient and prosperous enterprise.

Introduction

In the journey towards financial freedom, scaling your business is a pivotal step. It's the process of expanding your operations and increasing revenue without proportionately increasing costs. However, scaling requires careful planning, strategic decision-making, and the implementation of effective growth strategies. In this article, we'll delve into key strategies for scaling your business successfully.

Understanding Scaling

Scaling a business involves more than just increasing sales or hiring more employees. It's about optimizing processes, leveraging resources efficiently, and tapping into new markets while maintaining the essence of your brand and the quality of your offerings.

Establish Clear Goals

Before embarking on the journey of scaling, it's essential to establish clear and realistic goals. These goals should be specific, measurable, achievable, relevant, and time-bound (SMART). Whether it's expanding into new markets, launching new products, or increasing market share, having defined objectives provides a roadmap for growth.

Invest in Infrastructure

To support growth, it's crucial to invest in the infrastructure of your business. This includes upgrading technology systems, enhancing operational efficiency, and optimizing supply chain management. *Supply chain management* involves the planning, design, execution, control, and monitoring of activities involved in the flow of goods, services, information, and finances from the point of origin to the point of consumption, aiming to optimize efficiency, cost-effectiveness, and customer satisfaction throughout the entire supply chain network. A robust infrastructure provides the foundation for scalability and ensures that your business can handle increased demands without compromising quality or customer satisfaction.

Leverage Technology

In today's digital age, technology plays a pivotal role in scaling businesses. From cloud-based solutions to automation tools, technology can streamline processes, improve productivity, and enhance customer experiences. Embracing technological advancements enables businesses to operate more efficiently and adapt to changing market dynamics more effectively.

Focus on Customer Experience

A key driver of business growth is delivering exceptional customer experiences. By focusing on customer satisfaction, businesses can build brand loyalty, generate positive word-of-mouth referrals, and foster long-term relationships with clients. Investing in customer service training, soliciting feedback, and implementing customer-centric policies are essential for creating memorable experiences that drive growth.

Expand Marketing Efforts

Effective marketing is essential for scaling your business and reaching new audiences. Leveraging digital marketing channels such as social media, search engine optimization (SEO), and content marketing can increase brand visibility and attract potential customers. Additionally, targeted advertising campaigns and strategic partnerships can help businesses penetrate new markets and expand their customer base.

Foster a Culture of Innovation

To stay ahead of the competition and drive sustainable growth, businesses must foster a culture of innovation. Encouraging creativity, empowering employees to take calculated risks, and embracing new ideas are essential for fostering innovation within organizations. By continuously adapting and evolving, businesses can identify new opportunities for growth and remain relevant in a rapidly changing marketplace.

Diversify Revenue Streams

Relying solely on one product or service can be risky, especially in volatile economic environments. Diversifying revenue streams mitigates risks and creates multiple sources of income for businesses. Whether it's introducing new product lines, expanding into adjacent markets, or offering complementary services, diversification strengthens business resilience and enhances long-term sustainability.

Build Strategic Partnerships

Strategic partnerships can be instrumental in accelerating business growth and expanding market reach. By collaborating with complementary businesses or industry leaders, businesses can tap into new customer segments, access additional resources, and leverage existing networks. Strategic partnerships also provide opportunities for knowledge sharing, innovation, and mutual growth.

Monitor Key Performance Indicators (KPIs)

Tracking key performance indicators (KPIs) is essential for measuring the effectiveness of scaling strategies and identifying areas for improvement. Whether it's revenue growth, customer acquisition costs, or customer retention rates, monitoring KPIs provides valuable insights into business performance and informs decision-making processes. By analyzing data and adjusting strategies accordingly, businesses can optimize performance and drive sustainable growth.

Stay Agile and Adaptive

In today's fast-paced business environment, agility and adaptability are key to successful scaling. Markets evolve, consumer preferences change, and new technologies emerge rapidly. Businesses that can adapt quickly to shifting dynamics and seize opportunities are better positioned to thrive in dynamic environments. Staying agile allows businesses to pivot strategies, experiment with new approaches, and stay ahead of the curve.

Conclusion

Scaling a business requires careful planning, strategic execution, and a commitment to continuous improvement. By establishing clear goals, investing in infrastructure, leveraging technology, and focusing on customer experience, businesses can position themselves for sustainable growth and long-term success. By embracing innovation, diversifying revenue streams, and building strategic partnerships, businesses can unlock new opportunities and achieve financial freedom in the ever-evolving marketplace. Remember, scaling is not just about expanding operations; it's about creating value, making an impact, and realizing the full potential of your business.

Introduction

In the pursuit of financial freedom through entrepreneurship, setbacks and failures are inevitable companions along the journey. The path to success is not a linear one; it's often marked by twists, turns, and unexpected hurdles. However, it's not the failures themselves that define our journey but rather how we respond to them. Embracing failure and learning from setbacks are essential components of building resilience in the face of adversity.

Understanding Failure as a Catalyst for Growth

Failure is not the opposite of success; it's a stepping stone toward it. Many of the world's most successful entrepreneurs and business leaders have experienced numerous failures before achieving their goals. What sets them apart is their ability to view failure not as a setback but as an opportunity for growth and learning.

When we embrace failure, we shift our perspective from viewing it as a personal flaw to recognizing it as a natural part of the learning process. Each failure provides valuable insights into what works and what doesn't, allowing us to refine our strategies and approaches moving forward. By reframing failure as a catalyst for growth, we empower ourselves to extract valuable lessons from every setback.

Cultivating Resilience in the Face of Adversity

Resilience is the ability to adapt and bounce back in the face of challenges. It's a trait that is cultivated through experience and strengthened by adversity. In the world of entrepreneurship, resilience is often the differentiating factor between those who persevere and those who falter in the face of setbacks.

Building resilience begins with developing a growth mindset - the belief that our abilities and intelligence can be developed through dedication and hard work. With a growth mindset, setbacks are seen as temporary setbacks rather than insurmountable obstacles. This mindset shift enables us to approach challenges with optimism and perseverance, knowing that failure is not the end but merely a detour on the path to success.

Embracing Risk-Taking and Innovation

Entrepreneurship inherently involves risk-taking and innovation. It requires stepping outside of our comfort zones, taking calculated risks, and challenging the status quo. However, with risk comes the possibility of failure. Embracing failure means being willing to take risks, knowing that failure is a natural byproduct of pushing boundaries and exploring new opportunities.

Innovation thrives in environments where failure is not only accepted but embraced as a necessary part of the creative process. Some of the most groundbreaking discoveries and inventions have come as a result of countless failed attempts and experiments. By encouraging a culture of experimentation and risk-taking, entrepreneurs can foster a spirit of innovation that drives their businesses forward.

Learning from Setbacks

Reflection is a powerful tool for learning from setbacks and failures. Taking the time to reflect on our experiences allows us to gain insights into what went wrong, what could have been done differently, and what lessons can be applied to future endeavors.

When faced with a setback, resist the urge to dwell on the negative emotions associated with failure. Instead, approach the situation with curiosity and a willingness to learn. Ask yourself probing questions such as:

- ❖ What factors contributed to the setback?
- ❖ What were the warning signs that may have been overlooked?
- ❖ What actions can be taken to prevent similar setbacks in the future?

By engaging in reflective practices, we can extract valuable nuggets of wisdom from even the most challenging experiences.

Building a Support Network

Entrepreneurship can be a lonely journey, especially during times of adversity. Having a strong support network can provide much-needed encouragement, guidance, and perspective during difficult times. Surround yourself with mentors, peers, and advisors who understand the challenges of entrepreneurship and can offer support and mentorship when needed.

Seek out networking opportunities, join industry groups, and participate in entrepreneurship communities both online and offline. By connecting with others who share similar experiences and aspirations, you can gain valuable insights, perspective, and encouragement that can help you navigate the ups and downs of entrepreneurship with greater resilience and confidence.

Conclusion

Embracing failure and learning from setbacks are essential skills for building resilience in the world of entrepreneurship. By reframing failure as a catalyst for growth, cultivating a growth mindset, embracing risk-taking and innovation, engaging in reflective practices, and building a strong support network, entrepreneurs can navigate the challenges of entrepreneurship with resilience, perseverance, and optimism. Remember, it's not the setbacks themselves that define our journey but rather how we respond to them that ultimately shapes our path to success and financial freedom.

Introduction

In today's rapidly changing business landscape, the concept of sustainability has emerged as a crucial factor for long-term success and viability. Gone are the days when profit maximization was the sole focus of businesses. Increasingly, consumers, investors, and regulators are demanding that companies adopt sustainable practices that not only ensure profitability but also contribute positively to society and the environment. In this article, we will explore the importance of sustainable practices and how businesses can effectively balance profit with social responsibility.

Understanding Sustainability in Business

Sustainability in business encompasses a broad range of practices aimed at minimizing negative environmental impacts, promoting social equity, and ensuring economic viability for both present and future generations. It goes beyond mere compliance with regulations and involves proactive efforts to integrate environmental, social, and governance (ESG) considerations into business operations and decision-making processes.

At its core, sustainable business practices seek to strike a delicate balance between economic prosperity, social welfare, and environmental stewardship. This balance requires businesses to adopt a holistic approach that takes into account the interconnectedness of economic, social, and environmental systems.

The Triple Bottom Line: Profit, People, Planet

The concept of the triple bottom line (TBL) serves as a guiding framework for sustainable business practices. Developed by business scholar John Elkington in the 1990s, the TBL emphasizes three dimensions of performance: profit, people, and planet. Instead of focusing solely on financial outcomes, businesses embracing the TBL approach strive to create value across all three dimensions.

Profit represents the economic dimension and refers to the financial viability and profitability of the business. While generating profits is essential for the survival and growth of any enterprise, it should not come at the expense of social or environmental well-being.

The "people" aspect of the TBL emphasizes the importance of social responsibility and human well-being. This includes considerations such as labor practices, employee welfare, diversity and inclusion, community engagement, and respect for human rights. Sustainable businesses prioritize the welfare and empowerment of their employees, customers, and communities.

Lastly, the "planet" dimension focuses on environmental sustainability and stewardship. It involves minimizing resource consumption, reducing pollution and greenhouse gas emissions, conserving biodiversity, and promoting renewable energy and sustainable practices throughout the supply chain.

Integrating Social Responsibility into Business Strategy

Achieving sustainability requires a fundamental shift in the way businesses conceptualize and execute their strategies.

It involves embedding social and environmental considerations into all aspects of the business, from product design and sourcing to production, distribution, and marketing.

One effective way to integrate social responsibility into business strategy is through the adoption of sustainability frameworks and standards. Initiatives such as the United Nations Global Compact, the Sustainable Development Goals (SDGs), and the Global Reporting Initiative (GRI) provide guidance and benchmarks for businesses seeking to align their operations with sustainable principles.

Moreover, businesses can leverage technology and innovation to drive sustainability across their value chains. This may involve implementing energy-efficient practices, adopting renewable energy sources, optimizing resource utilization, and investing in green technologies and solutions. By embracing innovation, businesses can reduce their environmental footprint while also enhancing operational efficiency and competitiveness.

Collaboration and Partnerships for Impact

Collaboration and partnerships play a crucial role in advancing sustainability goals. No single organization can address complex societal and environmental challenges alone. By collaborating with stakeholders across sectors, businesses can leverage collective expertise, resources, and influence to drive positive change at scale.

Partnerships between businesses, governments, non-profit organizations, academia, and civil society can facilitate knowledge sharing, capacity building, and joint problem-solving efforts. Through multi-stakeholder initiatives and industry alliances, businesses can address shared challenges such as climate change, poverty alleviation, gender equality, and access to education and healthcare.

Furthermore, businesses can engage with their suppliers, customers, and other stakeholders to promote transparency and accountability throughout the value chain. By promoting responsible sourcing practices, ethical labor standards, and sustainable consumption patterns, businesses can create a ripple effect that extends beyond their immediate sphere of influence.

Measuring and Reporting Progress

Effective measurement and reporting are essential for tracking progress and demonstrating accountability in sustainability efforts. Businesses need to establish clear metrics, targets, and Key Performance Indicators (KPIs) to assess their performance across economic, social, and environmental dimensions.

Tools such as sustainability reporting frameworks, environmental impact assessments, and stakeholder engagement surveys can help businesses evaluate their performance, identify areas for improvement, and communicate their progress to stakeholders transparently. *Sustainability reporting frameworks* are structured guidelines and standards that organizations follow to transparently disclose their environmental, social, and governance (ESG) performance and impacts to stakeholders, facilitating accountability and transparency in corporate sustainability practices. *Environmental impact assessments* are comprehensive evaluations conducted to analyze and assess the potential environmental consequences of proposed projects, policies, or activities, aiding decision-making processes and ensuring sustainable development practices. *Stakeholder engagement surveys* are structured questionnaires or tools used to solicit feedback, opinions, and insights from various stakeholders, including customers, employees, investors, and community members, to inform decision-making and improve relationships between organizations and their stakeholders.

In addition to quantitative metrics, qualitative indicators such as stakeholder perceptions, reputation, and brand value are also important measures of sustainability success. Businesses that prioritize integrity, trust, and ethical conduct are more likely to build enduring relationships with customers, employees, investors, and communities.

Conclusion

Sustainable practices are no longer a luxury but a necessity for businesses seeking long-term success and relevance in a rapidly evolving world. By embracing the principles of sustainability and social responsibility, businesses can create value not only for their shareholders but also for society and the planet as a whole.

Balancing profit with social responsibility requires a strategic mindset, a commitment to innovation, and a willingness to collaborate and adapt to changing societal and environmental dynamics. As businesses navigate the complexities of the 21st century marketplace, they have a unique opportunity to lead by example and drive positive change for the benefit of present and future generations.

By integrating sustainability into their DNA (fundamental characteristics, values, and practices deeply ingrained within the core operations, culture, and identity of businesses), businesses can not only mitigate risks and enhance resilience but also unlock new opportunities for growth, innovation, and competitive advantage. In doing so, they can fulfill their dual mandate of driving sustainable growth while also contributing to the well-being of people and the planet. As we look ahead to the future of business, one thing is clear: the path to sustainable prosperity is paved with purpose, resilience, and collective action.

Introduction

Exiting a business is a pivotal moment for any entrepreneur. Whether you're retiring, pursuing new ventures, or simply ready to move on, how you exit your business can have a profound impact on your financial future and the legacy you leave behind. In this chapter, we'll explore the importance of planning for your business exit, strategies for a successful transition, and how to build a lasting legacy that extends beyond your time as a business owner.

Understanding the Importance of Planning

Planning for the exit of your business should ideally begin long before you're ready to make the move. A well-thought-out exit strategy allows you to maximize the value of your business, minimize taxes, and ensure a smooth transition for employees, customers, and stakeholders. Without proper planning, exiting your business can be chaotic, resulting in lost value and unnecessary complications.

Assessing Your Options

There are several options to consider when planning your business exit. You may choose to sell your business to a third party, transfer ownership to a family member or key employee, merge with another company, or liquidate your assets. Each option comes with its own set of advantages and challenges, and the right choice depends on your unique circumstances, financial goals, and personal preferences.

Preparing Your Business for Sale

If you decide to sell your business, preparation is key. Prospective buyers will scrutinize every aspect of your business, from financial performance and operational efficiency to market potential and growth opportunities. Take the time to address any weaknesses and enhance the strengths of your business to maximize its appeal to potential buyers. This may involve improving financial records, streamlining operations, and strengthening customer relationships.

Seeking Professional Advice

Exiting your business is a complex process that requires careful planning and expert guidance. Consider enlisting the help of professionals such as business brokers, accountants, attorneys, and financial advisors who specialize in business transitions. These professionals can provide valuable insights, navigate legal and financial complexities, and help you achieve the best possible outcome for your business exit.

Considering Tax Implications

Tax considerations play a significant role in the business exit process. Depending on how you structure the sale or transfer of your business, you may be subject to capital gains taxes, income taxes, estate taxes, and other levies. By working closely with tax advisors and financial experts, you can develop tax-efficient strategies that help minimize your tax liability and preserve more of your wealth for retirement and other financial goals.

Creating a Succession Plan

For businesses that will continue operations after the owner's exit, succession planning is essential. A well-designed succession plan ensures a smooth transition of leadership and management responsibilities, maintains business continuity, and preserves the values and culture that define your company. Identify and groom potential successors early on, provide them with mentorship and training, and document key processes and procedures to facilitate a seamless handover of responsibilities.

Building a Lasting Legacy

Beyond financial considerations, exiting your business is an opportunity to leave a lasting legacy. Consider the impact your business has had on employees, customers, suppliers, and the community at large. How can you ensure that your legacy endures long after you've moved on? This may involve documenting your company's history, values, and achievements, supporting charitable causes that align with your mission, and mentoring the next generation of entrepreneurs.

Transitioning to Life After Business

Exiting your business marks the beginning of a new chapter in your life. Transitioning from full-time entrepreneurship to retirement or other pursuits can be both exciting and challenging. Take the time to envision your post-business life, set new goals and priorities, and explore opportunities for personal and professional growth. Consider how you will stay engaged, fulfilled, and financially secure in retirement, whether through hobbies, travel, volunteering, or continued involvement in the business community.

Conclusion

Exiting your business is a significant milestone that requires careful planning, thoughtful consideration, and expert guidance. By taking proactive steps to prepare for your business exit, you can maximize value, minimize risk, and leave a lasting legacy that extends far beyond your time as a business owner. Whether you're retiring, pursuing new ventures, or simply ready for a change, the key is to approach your business exit with foresight, intention, and a clear vision for the future.

"Choosing the Right Business for Financial Freedom" is a comprehensive guide that navigates aspiring entrepreneurs through the intricate landscape of business ownership. From evaluating one's entrepreneurial mindset and passions to understanding market dynamics and risk assessment, each chapter offers invaluable insights into the multifaceted journey of entrepreneurship.

Spanning critical topics such as business models, financing, legal compliance, team building, branding, and scalability, this book equips readers with the essential tools and strategies needed to embark on a successful business venture. With a focus on sustainability, innovation, and resilience, "Choosing the Right Business for Financial Freedom" is not just a roadmap to financial independence but also a blueprint for building a purposeful and enduring legacy in the business world.

ABOUT THE AUTHOR

Mr. C. P. Kumar is a retired Scientist 'G' from National Institute of Hydrology, Roorkee, Uttarakhand, India. He is also a Reiki Healer and Chakra Balancing practitioner (with pendulum dowsing) and offers Emotional Freedom Technique (EFT) to help individuals with emotional issues. Mr. Kumar has authored many books on technical, spiritual, and social topics.

For further details, you may visit his webpage
https://www.angelfire.com/nh/cpkumar/virgo.html